A BRIEF ILLUSTRATED
HISTORY of
WARFARE

STEVE PARKER
&
DAVID WEST

raintree

a Capstone company — publishers for children

Published by Raintree, an imprint of Capstone Global Library Limited, 2017.
Raintree is an imprint of Capstone Global Library Limited, a company incorporated in England and Wales
having its registered office at 264 Banbury Road, Oxford, OX2 7DY –
Registered company number: 6695582
www.raintree.co.uk
myorders@raintree.co.uk

Designed and illustrated by David West
Text by Steve Parker
Editor Brenda Haugen
Produced by
David West Children's Books, 6 Princeton Court, 55 Felsham Road, London SW15 1AZ
Printed and bound in China

ISBN: 978-1-4747-2702-0 (hardcover)
20 19 18 17 16
10 9 8 7 6 5 4 3 2 1

British Library Cataloguing in Publication Data
A full catalogue record for this book is available from the British Library.

Every effort has been made to contact copyright holders of material reproduced in this book. Any
omissions will be rectified in subsequent printings if notice is given to the publisher.

CONTENTS

INTRODUCTION

About 4,300 years ago in Sumer (now Iraq) and other parts of west Asia, Sargon the Great founded an empire called Akkadia. He had the first full-time, professional army.

LONG AGO, PEOPLE LIVED IN SMALL GROUPS AS WANDERERS. THEY HAD FEW POSSESSIONS AND LITTLE TO DEFEND, AND AVOIDED CONFLICT BY MOVING ON. From about 12,000 years ago, farming and settlements – from small villages to towns and cities – produced buildings, crops and livestock that could be taken by force. As civilisations spread, people specialised in skilled professions such as farming, carpentry, pottery – and soldiering. Human desire for power, wealth, land and possessions led to the first armies. By 5,000 years ago, unorganised outbreaks of fighting had became organised warfare. The story has continued ever since, with technology playing a major role.

The first weapons of sticks and stones were shaped into clubs and spears, then adapted for bows, slings and catapults. Horse-drawn wheeled chariots increased mobility. Metals such as bronze and iron led to swords and axes, shields and armour. About 1,000 years ago, gunpowder's invention gave rise to bombs, canons, guns and missiles. New firearms spread through armies and navies and, in the 20th century, also into air forces with petrol engines, jets and rockets. World War I's (1914–1918) chemical weapons and World War II's (1939–1945) atomic bombs led to global treaties against mass death and suffering. But human desire for wealth and power remain, and new technologies bring more kinds of weapons. Every few years another war starts, and peace is put on hold.

From about 5,000 years ago in ancient Sumer, city-states – regions based around large settlements – battled for power and influence. The war between Lagash (formerly Sumer) and Umma, in 2525 BCE, is the first recorded in history in any detail. Victorious leader Eannatum of Lagash celebrated with a stele (carved stone slab) showing soldiers with spears, helmets and armour trampling the enemy (left). Weapons, armour, and army organisation and tactics advanced greatly over almost 2,000 years of regular fighting. Skilled archers on horseback used bows made of several strips of wood (below).

Frequent battles in Sumer over centuries led to many improvements in warfare. In this scene from about 4,500 years ago, infantry (soldiers on foot) charge across a plain. Four-wheeled chariots with solid wheels, pulled by asses native to the region, probably carried high-ranking leaders to the battlefield. They would get out to fight on foot – but perhaps reboard to make an escape if defeat loomed.

ANCIENT WARFARE
7TH CENTURY BCE – 168 BCE

FROM ABOUT 4,000 YEARS AGO, GREAT EMPIRES WERE BUILT IN EGYPT, THEN GREECE, WEST ASIA, INDIA AND CHINA. MOBILITY ADVANCED WITH EGYPTIAN WAR CHARIOTS. WEAPONRY EXPANDED WITH MORE KINDS OF BOWS, SLINGS, SWORDS, SPEARS AND ARMOUR. NEW BATTLE SYSTEMS INCLUDED THE GREEK PHALANX AND CAVALRY.

Ancient Egyptians used war chariots supported by infantry. It is said that semi-trained lions were set loose among the enemy.

Early warfare and the chariot

The first wheeled vehicles, such as carts and wagons, appeared in Sumer and other regions of west Asia more than 5,000 years ago. By 4,000 years ago, solid wheels on war chariots were being replaced by much lighter spoked wheels. This light two-wheeler was pulled by horses bred to be bigger and faster. It carried commanders, expert archers, spear-throwers, swordsmen and plentiful weapons swiftly around the battlefield. When on the move, it was difficult to stop or even attack. Chariots soon spread west to north Africa and east across Asia. They reached their peak around 3,500–3,000 years ago as the Egyptian pharoahs battled the Hittite empire (based in modern-day Turkey and Syria).

After that time, war chariots faded, although they were still used for races and parades. Their place was taken by soldiers on horseback, known as cavalry, armed with bows, swords and spears.

War at sea

Navies are 'armies on water'. At the time of ancient Greece, 2,600 years ago, naval battles had begun around the Mediterranean Sea. The main tactic was to ram the enemy boat so it sank or to come alongside and board the boat for hand-to-hand fighting. Sails failed if the wind fell or enemy vessels moved upwind, so rows of trained oarsmen were vital to manoeuvre into the best position.

A Greek trireme had three rows of oars as well as sails. It aimed a waterline metal ram at the bow (front) to pierce and sink opponents' ships.

The phalanx and light infantry

Weapons, armour and equipment are vital in warfare. So too are training, planning, organisation and tactics, with commanders giving orders that all troops obey. The main ancient Greek formation was the phalanx, in which rows of lightly armoured infantry (foot soldiers) formed a square that moved as one.

Greek slinger

Persian archer

Highly organised Greek phalanxes, bristling with spears behind a shield wall, marched straight at the enemy.

Their shields made a defensive wall as they jabbed with spears and pikes (long pointed poles). The phalanx could move into the midst of the enemy. Then, under orders, small groups broke away for lightning attacks and quickly returned to reform. Within the phalanx were archers, spear-throwers and slingers. The most successful Greek army leader, and one of the best war commanders of all time, was Alexander the Great (356–323 BCE).

Alexander leads a charge at the Battle of Issus in 333 BCE.

His phalanxes attacked the main opponents while his fast cavalry came in from the sides. Over dozens of battles, especially against Persians led by Darius, Alexander never lost. He established a vast empire stretching from Greece to India, but he died at only 32 years old, possibly from food poisoning.

Within a few years Alexander's empire fell apart. In 168 BCE the Greeks lost to the new superpower of the region – mighty Rome.

Greek hoplite with hoplon, helmet, spear and sword

Greek hoplite with metal thorax and greaves

Greek hoplite with linen thorax and decorated shield

Armour and war elephants

Greek foot soldiers were called hoplites from their hoplons or shields. They wore metal helmets, perhaps with faceplates. On their upper bodies they wore thoraxes of metal or thick layered material such as linen. Shinguard-type greaves protected their lower legs. However as Alexander's armies moved east across Asia, armour was ineffective against war elephants. These were used from perhaps 3,000 years ago in India and spread west to Europe.

Alexander's troops first faced Indian war elephants at the Battle of Gaugamela in 331 BCE.

THE ROMAN WAR MACHINE
4TH CENTURY BCE – 476 AD

NO EMPIRE HAS BEEN AS HUGE, LONG–LASTING, AND BASED ON MILITARY MIGHT, AS ANCIENT ROME. AT ITS HEIGHT THE ROMAN ARMY AND LOYAL FORCES IN ITS OCCUPIED TERRITORIES NUMBERED PERHAPS HALF A MILLION SOLDIERS. ADVANCES INCLUDED MACHINERY SUCH AS BALLISTAS, STRUCTURES INCLUDING FORTS AND WALLS, AND METHODS LIKE LAYING SIEGE TO TOWNS AND CITIES.

The Roman legionary

The Roman war machine was based on the legionary – a well–trained, fully-equipped, mobile professional soldier. The basic army unit was the legion of nearly 5,000 men. This was made up of 10 cohorts. A cohort contained six centuria, each of 80 men, led by a centurion. A centuria was further divided into 10 contubernia or basic fighting units of eight men. This organisation was very strict, and the leader at each level followed every order from above without question. Funding such an army was costly. The money came from taxes and selling produce and slaves, especially from each new region the Romans conquered.

On the march, a legionary carried all essentials for survival and battle. These included his shield, helmet, body armour, spare sandals, javelins, sword, dagger, rations (food) for two weeks, skin watercarrier, sarcina (marching pack) with cooking and eating equipment, wicker basket, shovel and two stakes to help, with others, to build a palisade (point-topped fence).

Roman infantry threw their javelins, then moved in for close combat with their swords.

Building an empire

The Roman empire had a shaky start, including defeats by the Senones of north Italy in 387 BCE. The Punic Wars between 264 and 146 BCE were three huge conflicts, the largest in the world at their time, with rival city-state Carthage across the Mediterranean in modern–day Tunisia. In 218 BCE, during the Second Punic War, brilliant Carthaginian general Hannibal crossed the Alps in north Italy with a fierce army and 30 war elephants.

Hannibal lost several elephants crossing the Alps.

Romans crushed all enemies.

For 15 years he won many local battles but failed to reach Rome. The Roman army showed no mercy in victory and when it finally took Carthage, it destroyed the city and killed or enslaved all of its people.

An onager fired large stones.

A ballista fired
small stones or large arrows.

Technologies and structures

Roman craftsmen devised many new weapons. The onager and ballista used energy stored in stretched or twisted wood and rope to fling heavy rocks, arrows or poles long distances. Flaming rag-bombs

also could be hurled into a besieged town. A development of the spear was the javelin, or pilum, designed to be thrown accurately over long distances to break up the enemy's formation. The gladius was a short double-edged sword made by welding strips of metal for strength yet lightness. It was ideal for stabbing and slashing. A longer version, up to one metre (3.3 feet), extended its range.

Vercingetorix, leader of the Gauls, surrenders to Rome's great military leader, Julius Caesar, at the Battle of Alesia in 52 BCE. The Romans built a wall 16 kilometres (11 miles) long around Alesia to stop people from getting out or supplies from getting in.

From their first major wars around 500 BCE, the Romans had invaded and conquered all lands around the Mediterranean by 100 BCE. They expanded in northern Europe, north Africa and west Asia, and by 100 AD ruled about one-fifth of the world's people. The empire ended in 476 AD when Germanic tribes overran the city.

Edge of the empire

The Roman empire was continually attacked around its edges, especially by the Gauls (in modern France) and Germanic peoples (in and around Germany). At the decisive Battle of Teutenberg Forest, an alliance of Germanic tribes halted the Romans' north-east spread at the Rhine River. In the north of England, the 6-metres (20-ft) high Hadrian's Wall marked the empire's northern limit. It was built and manned mainly by auxiliaries or part-time soldiers.

the Battle of Teutenberg Forest in 9 AD

Hadrian's Wall was completed in 128 AD.

RAIDERS AND INVADERS
476 – 1100

THE WESTERN ROMAN EMPIRE ENDED IN 476 AD, WHEN ROME ITSELF FELL TO REBELS AND THE LAST EMPEROR, ROMULUS AUGUSTUS, WAS REMOVED. THE 'DARK AGES' FOLLOWED AS TRIBES AND ARMIES BATTLED FOR POWER ACROSS EUROPE. THE EASTERN ROMAN OR BYZANTINE EMPIRE CONTINUED FOR ANOTHER 1,000 YEARS, BASED IN BYZANTIUM (CONSTANTINOPLE, NOW ISTANBUL).

Barbarian invasions of western Europe in the 5th century followed the Huns' attacks on Gothic kingdoms in 372–375.

Invading hordes

Romans called their enemies 'barbarians'. In north-east Europe during the 4th and early 5th centuries, the Goths, spreading south from Scandinavia, battled the Huns, who were moving west from central Asia under their legendary leader Attila. However the huge but poorly-ruled Hun empire faded after Attila's death in 453. The Goths split into two groups. The western Visigoths, along with

the Vandals who had also come from the north, dealt the final death blows to Rome and continued west to settle in Spain. The eastern Ostrogoths took from the Huns a huge area from Italy to the Black Sea. Battles were often decided by fast cavalry charges. The Huns were supreme riders and used composite bows, javelins, a long straight sword, slim dagger and lassoes. Meanwhile in west Asia, the Byzantine empire continued the Roman traditions of being highly organised and well defended.

The Byzantine empire survived many invasions due to its heavily armoured cavalry known as cataphracts.

With few horses in the far north, Vikings and other Norsemen fought mainly on foot.

Greek fire was used by the eastern Roman or Byzantine empire.

Greek fire

Despite its name, 'Greek' fire was used from the 670s by Byzantine naval forces, especially in the eastern Mediterranean and Black Sea. It burned ferociously and quickly torched enemy ships. Its chemical make-up is still a mystery.

10

At the Battle of Tours, 732, the Franks led by Charles Martel defeated the Islamic army of Abdul Rahman Al Ghafiqi.

Islam and the Franks

From the 620s the Islamic faith became established in what is now Saudi Arabia. In a series of religious conversions and military campaigns, within a century Islamic forces spread east to present-day Pakistan, north to the Black and Caspian seas, and west along north Africa and then through Spain into France. Near the city of Tours, the Islamic army came up against the Franks, a Germanic tribe who had taken over much of France after the Roman empire collapsed. The Islamic cavalry charged repeatedly but the battle-hardened Frankish infantry stood firm. With rumours that Franks were stealing the treasures the invaders had stolen, many Islamic soldiers left to save their loot. The battle reversed the spread of Islam in Europe.

The Normans

For centuries, Vikings and other Norse warriors from Scandinavia, in the far north, had raided the coasts of Britain and northern Europe. In the 10th century some settled in what is now Normandy, in north-west France. During the next century, they spread south to Italy, east toward Byzantium, and north into Britain under their leader William II 'the Conqueror'. They used a combination of heavily armed infantry, well-protected cavalry, and groups of archers who rained arrows down on to the enemy.

Norman knight

The Norman army of infantry, cavalry and archers defeated the English infantry at the Battle of Hastings in 1066.

A shield wall was used by English infantry at Hastings.

The shield wall

Used since ancient times, the shield wall consisted of infantry soldiers standing shoulder-to-shoulder, overlapping their shields to form a continuous barrier. Specialised observers watched the enemy closely and shouted orders so that the shields moved all together. For example, shields would be raised overhead for falling arrows, or soldiers would crouch down against javelins. Use of the tactic faded as rapid cavalry charges became more effective.

KNIGHTS AND CASTLES
1100 – 1452

a knight wearing plate armour

THE MIDDLE AND LATE MIDDLE AGES WAS A WORLD OF ARMOURED KNIGHTS AND STONE CASTLES IN EUROPE, AS BOTH REACHED THE PEAK OF THEIR DEVELOPMENT. MOUNTED KNIGHTS IN FULL ARMOUR WERE FORMIDABLE ENEMIES, BUT THEY WERE ULTIMATELY DEFEATED BY THE NEW WEAPONS AND TACTICS.

Christian knights on horseback battled with Islamic warriors during the third crusade (1189–1192).

Mounted knights and chivalry

During this period, armour developed from chainmail and small pieces of sheet metal to a suit of steel plate armour that covered a mounted knight from head to foot. With helmets that covered their faces, it was impossible to tell which knight was which in battle, so knights painted symbols on their shields to identify themselves. The surcoat, a sleeveless garment worn over the armour, was embroidered with the same symbols. This became known as a knight's coat of arms. Knights pledged to fight bravely according to a code of conduct known as chivalry. Christian knights fought in a series of wars in the Holy Land, called crusades. Their aim was to seize religious sites from Muslim rulers and protect pilgrims who visited them.

During a siege, machines called trebuchets flung projectiles weighing more than 50 kilogrammes (110 pounds) at castle walls up to 300 metres (1,000 ft) away.

Genghis Khan

Mongols fought mainly on horseback. For control, they used stirrups, which had been invented by the Huns but little used by others.

The Mongol empire

In 1206 in what is now Mongolia, Genghis Khan (1162–1227) united many local tribes and declared himself supreme leader. Over the next 20 years, his armies of fast, skilful riders – experts with the bow, lance and sword – spread out in all directions. Travelling with little more than weapons, armour and horses, they hunted wild animals for food and took whatever they needed from towns and villages. Anyone who protested was shown no mercy.

Unarmoured Swiss infantry armed with halberds defeated armoured Austrian knights at the Battle of Morgarten in Switzerland in 1315.

The rise of infantry

In the 14th and 15th centuries, foot-soldiers began to challenge the knights. They used pikes, long poles with sharp spear-tips, to fend off mounted knights, who were reluctant to ride into a line of pikemen. A similar long-reach weapon called the halberd, a pole with a metal spike and an axe-head on the end, could be used in the same way. One of the most effective ways to deal with knights on the battlefield was the use of massed bowmen. English longbowmen were trained from

longbowman

English longbowmen outranged the enemy and brought down many mounted French knights at the Battle of Crécy in 1346.

childhood and could shoot a dozen arrows a minute. They could put up a hail of arrows to stop a cavalry charge in its tracks. English archers were the key to almost every major victory in the Hundred Years' War (1337–1453) between England and France, from Crécy in 1346 to Agincourt in 1415.

But it was the development of the crossbow that finally ended the age of the knight. While the longbow required a lifetime of practice and great physical strength to master, crossbows could be used by untrained soldiers.

Joan of Arc led French infantry to a series of victories during the Hundred Years' War.

Mongols were skilled at besieging cities, such as Vladimir in eastern Russia in 1238.

The Mongol advance was so rapid and ferocious that few people could resist it. After the death of Genghis, his son Ogedei, and then Ogedei's son Kuyuk, continued the invasions. By 1260 the Mongols had conquered a vast area to create the largest single empire the world had ever seen. It stretched from Siberia southward to India, and eastward from eastern Europe to Japan, where the Mongol army met Japan's famous samurai warriors. The Mongol empire was eventually ruled by Genghis Khan's grandson Kublai Khan, but disputes broke out between family members, and the empire began falling apart around 1270.

samurai warrior

GUNPOWDER AND GUNS
1453 – 1750

EUROPE INTRODUCED CANNONS TO SMASH DOWN CASTLE WALLS AND SOW FEAR AND CONFUSION AMONG ARMIES. THE COMBINED USE OF MUSKETS AND PIKEMEN WITH CAVALRY SUPPORT BECAME THE NEW ORDER. MEANWHILE AT SEA, NAVAL WARFARE ADVANCED TOO.

Mehmed II and the Ottoman army attacked Constantinople in 1453 with a giant bombard.

The power of the gun

Gunpowder was invented in the 10th century in China. Chinese experimenters soon discovered that when gunpowder ignited inside a tube sealed at one end, a fiery jet exploded out of the open end. Then they found that these tubes could shoot out objects. They had invented the cannon. Cannons were being used in Europe by the 13th century. They may have been used at the siege of Seville in Spain in 1247–1248. Some early cannons were short, wide-barrelled weapons called bombards that hurled huge stone balls at castle walls.

Early cannons were small enough to be carried by one person. They evolved into long-barrelled handguns called arquebuses. Armies were quick to use them. Spanish forces with arquebuses defeated a bigger French army at the Battle of Cerignola in Italy in 1503. The arquebus evolved into the musket, which was used until the 18th century.

A musketeer stands ready for action.

Spanish conquistadors used muskets and cannons to defeat the Aztec empire in present-day Mexico in 1521.

Galleons

At sea, galleons were the dominant European fighting ships of the 16th to 18th centuries. They were longer and slimmer than cargo ships, making them fast and manoeuvrable. When the Spanish Armada attacked the English navy in 1588, the warships in both fleets were mainly galleons. They carried sails on three or four masts, and they were armed with cannons on two or more gundecks.

the Spanish Armada, 1588

A Spanish galleon fires at a Dutch warship in about 1618.

The Swedish king Gustavus Adolphus, portrayed here at the Battle of Breitenfeld in 1631, was famous for his innovative use of combined arms.

Combined arms

Military commanders knew that different weapons could be used together to achieve more than they could on their own. This is called combined arms. King Gustavus Adolphus of Sweden (1594–1632) used this principle to build one of the most effective armies in Europe. He had pikemen, musketeers and cavalry supported by artillery, all working together instead of fighting as separate units. His most famous victory was the Battle of Breitenfeld near Leipzig in Germany in 1631, during the Thirty Years' War (1618–1648). The battle was fought between the Protestant States and the Catholic League. Gustavus Adolphus led his combined forces to the first major Protestant victory of the war.

During the English Civil War (1642–1651), a combined arms tactic known as pike and shot was used to great effect. Three rows of musketeers lined up. The front row knelt, the middle row crouched and the back row stood, so that they could fire over each other. Pikemen amongst them held long pikes to protect the musketeers from cavalry charges.

Parliamentarians, armed with muskets during the English Civil War (1642–1651), were protected from cavalry charges by pikemen.

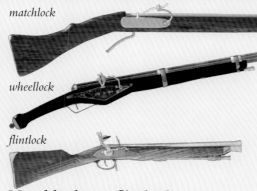

matchlock

wheellock

flintlock

Matchlocks to flintlocks

All handheld guns used the same basic technique – igniting a small pan of gunpowder on the gun to send a flash through a touch-hole and set off the gunpowder charge.

The matchlock was the first weapon of this type and was invented in about 1450. Pulling a lever lowered a smouldering cord into the pan of gunpowder and ignited it. The wheellock was invented in about 1500. Pulling the trigger spun a metal wheel against a rock, making sparks to ignite the gunpowder. The flintlock appeared in the 1600s.

Pulling the trigger released a lever with a piece of flint at the end. The flint struck a steel plate, creating sparks, as the pan of gunpowder was exposed so the sparks could ignite it.

Flintlock muskets were used by Swedish and Russian forces at the Battle of Poltava in 1726.

THE SEVEN YEARS' WAR
1755 – 1764

THE GROWING POWER OF BRITAIN AND PRUSSIA LED TO CONFLICT WITH OTHER EUROPEAN COUNTRIES AND THEIR OVERSEAS COLONIES. THE RESULT WAS THE FIRST GLOBAL WAR, THE SEVEN YEARS' WAR, SPANNING FOUR CONTINENTS. THE OUTCOME TRANSFORMED BRITAIN INTO THE WORLD'S LEADING MILITARY POWER.

British Major-General Robert Clive (centre) after the Battle of Plassey in India in 1757

England and the colonies

Skirmishes between French and British colonies in North America erupted into war in 1756. At first, the French were stronger, but Britain sent an army that ultimately won and drove out the French. A key British victory was the Battle of Quebec in 1759. Britain and France were also at war in India, where British forces under Robert Clive were victorious. This brought India under the control of the British.

The British commander, General James Wolfe, was killed in the attack on Quebec in 1759.

Warships pound each other at Quiberon Bay in 1759.

War in Europe

In Europe, the war raged across land and sea. British and Prussian forces scored victories at Prague (1757) in the modern-day Czech Republic, and Crefeld (1758) and Rossbach (1758) in Germany. The French fleet was also defeated at the Battle of Quiberon Bay (1759) in France. The war continued with more British–Prussian success until 1763.

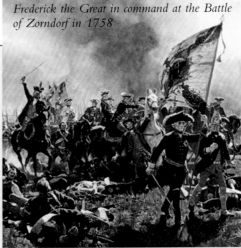

Frederick the Great in command at the Battle of Zorndorf in 1758

The bayonet

A knife or spike fixed to the end of a musket barrel was called a bayonet. It meant the musket could be used as a spear or pike. Early 'plug bayonets' were pushed into the end of the barrel. Later bayonets clipped to the barrel so that the musket could be fired with a bayonet in place.

fixed bayonets at the Battle of Culloden, 1745

Frederick the Great

King Frederick II of Prussia (1712–1786) is remembered as a great military tactician. He is famous for the oblique order attack, which concentrated an attack on one flank (side) of an enemy line. He also introduced light horse artillery units that could move guns quickly around a battlefield. Tactics like these enabled him to win battles where his forces were considerably outnumbered.

THE AMERICAN WAR OF INDEPENDENCE
1775 – 1783

IN THE 1770S, BRITAIN'S NORTH AMERICAN COLONIES GREW RESENTFUL AT STRICT LAWS AND HIGHER TAXES IMPOSED BY A GOVERNMENT IN BRITAIN, WHERE THE COLONIES HAD NO REPRESENTATIVES. PROTESTS TURNED TO VIOLENCE AND EVENTUALLY A REVOLUTION. BRITAIN FOUND ITSELF AT WAR WITH ITS OWN COLONIES TO DECIDE THE FATE OF THE CONTINENT.

Lexington, 1775

The war begins
Fighting broke out at Lexington, Massachusetts, on 19 April 1775, and quickly spread. The colonies formed an army under the command of George Washington.

On 4 July 1776, Britain's 13 American colonies declared independence. Troops arrived from Britain to quash the rebellion, and at first they succeeded.

The 1st Maryland Regiment used bayonet charges against the British at the Battle of Guilford Courthouse in 1781.

The 1781 Siege of Yorktown was the last major land battle of the American War of Independence.

Then Washington scored a famous victory at the Battle of Trenton in 1776, which encouraged the Americans to fight on. The war was fought mainly by foot-soldiers armed with muskets and cannons.

In 1777 a British invasion from Canada failed. American victories continued. Finally, British forces commanded by General Charles Cornwallis became trapped at Yorktown in 1782. Unable to escape, they surrendered when the French fleet stopped British ships from reaching the coast to rescue them. It was a catastrophe for the British that marked the end of the war. They saw that they could not win, and they withdrew their troops. The Treaty of Paris in 1783 formally ended the war.

European powers
The American War of Independence, also known as the American Revolutionary War, was not simply a war between Britain and its American colonies. France, Spain and the Netherlands entered the war as a way to achieve their own ends. France was keen to fight its old enemy, Britain, after losing the Seven Years' War. Spain hoped to recapture Gibraltar and Menorca from the British while they were busy with a war in America. The British offered to give west Florida to the Spanish if they stayed out of the war, but to no avail. The Dutch tried to stay neutral because they wanted to continue trading with the American colonies. However opponents of the Dutch leader, Willem V, supported the revolution. At first, European supporters gave the Americans money for the war, and then they sent arms, troops and warships. The French and Spanish fleets together outnumbered the British and tipped the balance of power against Britain.

Spanish troops at the Siege of Pensacola in 1781

REVOLUTIONARY AND NAPOLEONIC WARS
1792 – 1815

At the end of the 18th century, France, in the middle of its own revolution, fought a series of wars against Britain and partnerships of other countries. These wars brought a Corsican soldier called Napoleon Bonaparte to notice. He went on to lead the French army across Europe, until he was finally defeated at the Battle of Waterloo.

The French used a manned balloon at the Battle of Fleurus in 1794, to spy on the enemy from above. It was the first time an aerial craft influenced the result of a battle.

Napoleon's invasion of Russia in 1812 ended in disaster for his forces. His failed campaign cost the lives of 380,000 soldiers.

The Revolutionary Wars

The French invasion of the Austrian Netherlands in 1792 was the start of the Revolutionary Wars. Other European countries united against France, whose fortunes were mixed until armies commanded by Napoleon (1769–1821) won a series of decisive victories. Napoleon became a national hero. He returned to France, overthrew a weak government and declared himself emperor in 1804.

The Napoleonic Wars

Napoleon attempted to create a new continental empire by invading and conquering much of Europe. He defeated an Austro-Russian army at Austerlitz in 1805 and invaded Portugal in 1807 and Spain in 1808. He often attacked first with a small force, and then mounted a surprise main attack from the side or rear. But victory at sea eluded him. The French fleet was defeated by the British admiral Horatio Nelson at the Battle of Trafalgar in 1805. An alliance led by the Duke of Wellington and the Prussian field marshal Gebhard Leberecht von Blücher finally defeated Napoleon at the Battle of Waterloo in 1815.

The Peninsular War (1807–1814) was fought between Napoleon's forces and the combined powers of Spain, Britain and Portugal.

The Battle of Waterloo

Napoleon's battle tactics involved an artillery bombardment, followed by infantry and cavalry attacks. When the cavalry attacked, the British troops formed squares with bayonets pointing outward. The cavalry were supposed to withdraw, so the squares could be bombarded – but the French cavalry did not withdraw, taking terrible casualties from musket-fire and preventing the artillery from firing. Late-arriving Prussians helped the British and allied forces to win. The Battle of Waterloo was the last major battle fought in Europe by soldiers armed with swords, muskets and cannons.

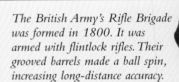

The British Army's Rifle Brigade was formed in 1800. It was armed with flintlock rifles. Their grooved barrels made a ball spin, increasing long-distance accuracy.

British troops formed defensive squares at Waterloo in 1815.

AMERICAN CIVIL WAR
1861 – 1865

The American Civil War saw advances in weaponry with larger howitzer artillery, the rapid-firing Gatling gun and the revolver. This new military technology contributed to the great numbers killed and wounded during the war. The war also featured the first naval battle between ships with ironclad hulls.

The United States at war

The American Civil War began in 1861 when the Confederate southern states attacked a Union Army fortress, Fort Sumter, near Charleston, South Carolina. After four years of intense fighting, the Union states in the north won, but more American soldiers were killed in the Civil War than in both world wars combined, making it the bloodiest war in US military history. The number of casualties was so high because of the new military technology used. Samuel Colt had produced the first successful, mass-produced revolver, the Colt Navy revolver, in 1851. It could fire six times before it had to be reloaded. It became the

The Battle of Gettysburg, 1863, was the turning point in the war.

the Colt Navy revolver, 1851

standard military handgun. Colt supplied guns to both sides during the Civil War.

The Union Army employed a terrifying weapon called a Gatling gun. It had six or more barrels fixed to a central shaft. Turning a handle spun the barrels. Each barrel fired once per revolution. The gun fired at a rate of about 400 rounds per minute.

Artillery, including 6-, 12- and 24-pounder field guns and howitzers, was used extensively. As well as solid shot, they could fire canisters filled with metal balls, nails or scrap iron. This 'canister shot' had a devastating effect.

Gatling gun

Ironclads

Soon after the Civil War began, the Confederacy decided to build armoured warships to give them an advantage over the more numerous Union warships. For their first experiment, they converted a wrecked ship, the *Merrimack*, into an ironclad warship, the CSS *Virginia*. The Union learned of the plan and built its own ironclad, the USS *Monitor*. The two strange-looking, low-lying ironclad ships met at the Battle of Hampton Roads, in 1862.

The two warships fought for about three hours to little effect. Shells fired by each ship bounced off the other.

Lessons taken from the battle later influenced the design of many other navies' ships and weapons.

The ironclads USS Monitor *and CSS* Virginia *fire at each other at Hampton Roads in 1862.*

EMPIRES AND RIFLES
1840 – 1902

BRITAIN HAD ESTABLISHED A WORLDWIDE EMPIRE THAT NEEDED TO BE GOVERNED AND PROTECTED. INDIA, KNOWN AS THE 'JEWEL OF THE EMPIRE', WAS THE MOST IMPORTANT PART. MEANWHILE IN EUROPE, A NEW GERMAN EMPIRE WAS ON THE RISE. MILITARY TECHNOLOGY PRODUCED NEW WEAPONS THAT WERE MORE POWERFUL, ACCURATE AND DEADLY.

The grease on the paper cartridges for the new rifles used by Indian soldiers in the British Army in India was one of the reasons for the Indian Mutiny of 1857.

The British in India

Local people who served as soldiers in India under British commanders were known as sepoys. The sepoys rebelled in 1857. One reason was the new Enfield P53 rifle. To load it, they had to bite the end off a paper cartridge. The paper was greased with beef and pork fat, which offended Hindus and Muslims. Since many sepoys were Hindus and Muslims, they refused to use it. The rebellion was eventually put down but cost thousands of lives.

War in Africa

During the 19th century, the European powers rushed to seize parts of Africa to add to their empires. It was known as the 'scramble for Africa'. The result was a series of wars across the continent. They included the Anglo–Zulu War against the Zulu Kingdom in southern Africa, two Boer Wars against Dutch-speaking settlers in southern Africa, and the Anglo–Egyptian War against Egyptian and Sudanese forces. Nearly all resulted in British victories.

One reason for the British successes in African wars was superior weaponry. British troops were armed with the breech-loading Martini–Henry rifle. It was accurate up to about 914 metres (3,000 ft).

The British Martini–Henry was a breech-loading rifle. It entered service in 1871. It was quicker to load and had a longer range than existing muzzle loaders. British forces used them in the Anglo-Zulu War in 1879.

Martini-Henry rifle

European wars

After the Napoleonic Wars, Europe was largely peaceful for the next hundred years. One exception was the Crimean War. It began with a Russian attack on the Turkish fleet at the Battle of Sinop in 1853. Britain and France joined forces with Turkey against Russia. Advances in military technology boosted the firepower available. Rifles were now beginning to replace muskets.

Spiral grooves in the barrel made a bullet spin, making it more accurate. Early rifles, such as the French Minié, were muzzle loaders. These were replaced by breech loaders. The cartridge was inserted at the rear end.

The muzzle-loading Minié rifle was one of the most accurate and deadly infantry weapons of the mid-19th century.

the tragic Charge of the Light Brigade during the Crimean War (1854–1855)

Garibaldi and his redshirts fought at the Battle of Calatafimi in 1860.

At the Battle of Omdurman in 1898, a highly disciplined British army equipped with modern rifles, machine guns and artillery defeated a Sudanese warrior force twice its size.

Soldiers no longer had to load the gunpowder charge and lead ball separately. The Martini-Henry fired a cartridge that contained the charge and the bullet. Once fired, pulling a lever would eject the spent cartridge.

The British also had the Maxim machine gun. As each round fired, some of its energy was used to eject the spent cartridge and load the next round. The Maxim could fire 600 rounds a minute, and it kept firing as long as the trigger was pressed.

The Boers were highly mobile and skilled marksmen.

the Sino-Japanese War (1894–1895)

The Far East

In the Far East, friction between China and Japan over control of Korea led to the first Sino-Japanese War of 1894–1895. Since Japan's navy was modelled on the British Royal Navy and their army on those of France and Germany, Japan was victorious against poorly organised Chinese forces.

Increased foreign involvement in China caused resentment among the Chinese people and led to an uprising called the Boxer Rebellion (1899–1901). It was eventually put down by 20,000 troops sent by an alliance of eight western nations.

American troops fought in Peking, China, during the Boxer Rebellion.

Rise of the German empire

During the 19th century, Prussia and the other German states came together to become a unified German empire, the forerunner of the modern German state. The new empire had a lot of industry and rapidly became one of Europe's great powers. French opposition to the unification of the German states led to the Franco-Prussian War (1870–1871). The biggest conflict of the war was the Battle of Gravelotte in 1870. The war resulted in a Prussian victory, and spurred the last German states to join the empire. The rise of a powerful Germany and the fears of other European states sowed the seeds of World War I, also known as the Great War.

French and Prussian forces met in combat at the Battle of Gravelotte in 1870.

WORLD WAR I
1914 – 1918

A WAR OF UNPARALLELED SCALE AND DEVASTATION BROKE OUT IN EUROPE IN 1914. MUCH OF THE WAR WAS FOUGHT BY SOLDIERS IN TRENCHES AND INVOLVED THE MASSIVE USE OF ARTILLERY. IT ALSO FEATURED THE FIRST WIDESPREAD USE OF SUBMARINES, TANKS AND AIRCRAFT IN A MAJOR WAR. MODERN CHEMICAL WEAPONS WERE USED TOO.

Ranks of artillery fired together at one area in an attack called an artillery barrage. It was often used to protect soldiers as they advanced.

War breaks out

The assassination of Archduke Franz Ferdinand of Austria in Sarajevo (now in Bosnia-Herzegovina) on 28 June 1914 triggered a series of events that led to the most destructive war the world had ever seen. It became known as the Great War. Before the end of the year, Austria's ally, Germany, was at war with Britain and France in the west and with Russia in the east. The war drew in soldiers, sailors and airmen from many other countries in Europe and from around the world, including Australia, New Zealand, the United States, India and Japan.

The armies fighting on the Western Front (to Germany's west) lived in trenches dug in the ground to protect them from enemy fire. During an attack, artillery bombarded the enemy trenches. Then the troops climbed up out of their trenches and walked toward the enemy. If the bombardment

Within months, trench warfare dominated the fighting in many places (left).

Chemical weapons, such as chlorine gas and mustard gas, caused thousands of casualties during the war (right).

Air warfare

Balloons, airships and planes had already been used in other wars, but the Great War was the first to employ aircraft in large numbers. At first, they were scouts that spied on enemy troops and artillery. By the end of the war, the first air forces were flying purpose-built fighters and bombers. Most were biplanes, with two wings, one above the other. The fighters, armed with machine guns, engaged in aerial battles called dogfights. The best pilots were known as air aces.

British fighters battle with German aircraft in a dogfight over the Western Front.

Machine guns were very effective against infantry advancing across a battlefield.

was ineffective, the soldiers walked into lethal enemy fire. Miles of barbed wire laid across the land also made it difficult for soldiers to advance. The Eastern Front was different from the Western Front. It was far longer – almost 1,600 km (1,000 miles) from the Baltic to the Black Sea, and the battle lines continually moved, making trenches impractical.

New weapons

On 15 September 1916, during the Battle of Flers-Courcelette, German troops saw strange vehicles lumbering toward them from the British lines. They were the first tanks ever seen in battle. They drove straight over barbed wire and trenches, and bullets bounced off them. They were slow and often broke down, but other countries started to build them and to develop new anti-tank weapons.

Chemical weapons were used for the first time too. Although international agreements outlawed them, all the major armies used them. They usually took the form of poisonous gas. Once released into the air, the gas presented a serious danger to both soldiers and civilians as it blew across the land.

Tanks were introduced to try to break the stand-off that trench warfare had created on the Western Front.

The number of war casualties was enormous. On only the first day of the Battle of the Somme, 20,000 British and 12,000 German soldiers were killed. The war ended in victory for the Allies. By then about 20 million people were dead, half of them military and half civilian.

War at sea

The war at sea was dominated by big battleships called dreadnoughts, and submarines. The only major sea battle was the Battle of Jutland in 1916.

The HMS Dreadnought was built in 1906.

The British Royal Navy had cut off all sea routes through the North Sea to Germany, so the German fleet was keen to open the seaways again. At the end of the battle, both navies claimed victory. Germany had sunk more ships, but Britain was still in control of the North Sea.

Germany had fewer warships than Britain, so they used submarines to gain an advantage. German submarines, called U-boats, sank enemy warships and cargo ships. Passenger ships thought to be

carrying war supplies were attacked by U-boats too. One of them was the RMS *Lusitania*. It was sunk in 1915 off the coast of Ireland – 1,200 lives were lost.

A U-boat surfaces alongside a sinking ship.

WORLD WAR II
1939 – 1945

BARELY 20 YEARS AFTER THE END OF THE GREAT WAR, GERMANY WAS INVOLVED IN ANOTHER GLOBAL WAR. FIGHTING RAGED FOR SIX YEARS AND INVOLVED ALL OF THE WORLD'S MAJOR MILITARY POWERS AND THREE CONTINENTS. IT WAS THE DEADLIEST CONFLICT IN HUMAN HISTORY (SO FAR), WITH MORE THAN 50 MILLION FATALITIES.

War in Europe and North Africa

World War II began on 1 September 1939, when German troops invaded Poland. Britain and France declared war on Germany. More and more countries were brought into the conflict until it became another global war. An invasion of Britain seemed inevitable in 1940, but Germany needed control of the air space over Britain before they could mount a land attack. The German air force, called the Luftwaffe, lost this aerial conflict – the Battle of Britain – which was the first clash ever fought entirely by air forces. Germany then began an intense bombing campaign against British cities, known as the Blitz. By 1941, Germany had conquered most of Europe.

A German tactic called blitzkrieg was an intense, fast attack using armour, highly mobile infantry and close air support.

If Germany had won the Battle of Britain in 1940, a land invasion of Britain would have followed.

Germany and its main allies, Italy and Japan, (the Axis Powers), seemed unstoppable. Then in December 1941, Japan attacked the US Navy at Pearl Harbor in Hawaii, and the United States entered the war. The Allies (Britain, the United States and the Soviet Union) finally halted

U-boats and the Battle of the Atlantic

Germany used U-boats even more effectively than in the Great War. Groups of U-boats, known as wolf packs, patrolled the Atlantic Ocean searching for convoys of Allied ships and sinking them. The cat and mouse chase between the Allied ships and German submarines, surface ships and aircraft was known as the Battle of the Atlantic. The Allies eventually won with a combination of new weapons and tactics and by breaking the German codes used to send radio messages to and from the U-boats.

Thousands of Allied ships, mostly merchant ships, were attacked and sunk by U-boats during the Battle of the Atlantic, 1939–1945.

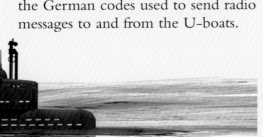

a V-1 missile, nicknamed 'Doodlebug' (above) and a V-2 rocket (right)

Secret weapons

German weapons developed during the war included the V-1 jet-powered missile and the V-2, which was rocket-powered. Thousands of both missiles rained down on Allied cities.

the Axis Powers in 1942–1943 at El Alamein in north Africa and Stalingrad in the Soviet Union. The Allied operations continued with the invasion of Italy in 1943.

On 6 June 1944, the Allies carried out the biggest seaborne invasion in history, known as D-Day. Thousands of ships and planes landed 156,000 troops on the coast of Normandy in northern France. They fought their way inland and kept going until they, and Soviet troops advancing from the east, reached Berlin, Germany's capital, in April 1945. German leader Adolf Hitler killed himself, and Germany soon surrendered. The war in Europe was over, but the fighting continued in the Pacific.

Japanese Zero fighters and American Grumman Wildcats met each other in combat over the Pacific Ocean during the Battle of Midway in 1942.

Japanese progress across the Pacific was finally halted by a United States victory at the Battle of Midway in 1942. Allied operations switched from defence to attack at the Battle of Guadalcanal in 1942–1943. As the Allies battled across the Pacific, Japanese forces fought hard to hold each island, but the Allies prevailed. In desperation, Japan sent suicide pilots on 'kamikaze' missions to fly their planes into Allied warships. The Pacific War finally ended when Japan was attacked with atomic bombs. It had been the greatest maritime conflict in history.

Troops wade ashore in Normandy on D-Day.

War in the Pacific

In the years before World War II, Japan had built up a formidable navy of battleships, aircraft carriers and long-range submarines. After Pearl Harbor, Japan rapidly occupied a huge area of the Pacific to add to the conquests on land it had made during the 1930s.

American Marines fought hotly contested battles on one island after another during the Pacific War.

The most destructive secret weapon of the war was the atomic bomb, or A–bomb. Fears that Germany might develop atomic weapons prompted the Allies to create their own A-bomb.

The top-secret project was code-named the Manhattan Project.

By the time the bomb was ready, the war in Europe was almost over, but the Pacific War was still ferocious. Faced with enormous casualties if Japan had to be invaded by troops, the Allies chose to attack Japanese cities with atomic weapons in 1945. After Hiroshima and Nagasaki had been destroyed, killing more than 100,000 civilians, Japan finally surrendered, bringing World War II to an end.

the A-bomb cloud over Nagasaki on 9 August 1945

THE COLD WAR ERA
1945 – 1989

IN THE DECADES AFTER WORLD WAR II, THE RIVALRY BETWEEN THE UNITED STATES AND THE USSR (SOVIET UNION) CAUSED TENSION AND CONFLICT. IT WAS A PERIOD KNOWN AS THE COLD WAR. MOST OF EUROPE ENJOYED PEACE, BUT BATTLES CONTINUED TO FLARE UP ELSEWHERE. WAR IN THIS PERIOD INCREASINGLY FEATURED JET AIR POWER AND GUIDED MISSILES.

The Chinese Civil War began in 1927 and did not end until 1950 – a year after the establishment of the People's Republic of China.

The rise of communism

The first communist state, the Soviet Union, was established in 1922 after a revolution ended tsarist rule in Russia. Then in 1947 civil war broke out in China between communist forces and the ruling nationalist party, or Kuomintang. The communists won in 1949 and established the People's Republic of China under the leadership of Mao Zedong.

Lines in the sand

Jewish communities in Europe were almost destroyed by Nazi Germany's attempt to wipe out Europe's Jews during World War II. Many of the survivors fled to Palestine in the Holy Land after the war. In 1948, the Jewish state of Israel was established in place of Palestine. The surrounding Arab countries opposed Israel, leading to a series of Arab-Israeli wars, Arab uprisings and terrorist campaigns that have continued to the present day.

The major wars include the First Arab-Israeli War of 1948-1949, the Six-Day War in 1967, and the Yom Kippur War in 1973. Much of Israel and the surrounding land is desert or rolling hills – an ideal environment for tanks, which have often featured prominently in Israel's wars. Israel has developed its own unique tank, the Merkava. It is thought that Israel may have developed nuclear weapons too, but this has not been confirmed. There have been many efforts to solve the Arab-Israeli conflict since 1948.

Israel has fought eight wars to defend itself since it became an independent country in 1948.

Jet combat

The first jet fighter was the Messerschmitt Me-262, developed by Germany at the end of World War II. It was too late to change the outcome of the war, but its abilities led all major air forces to develop their own jet fighters.

American P-80 Shooting Stars, F-94 Starfires, F9F Panthers and F-86 Sabres met Soviet MiG-15 jets in combat during the Korean War. They were heavily armed and fast, flying just under the speed of sound.

The Korean War was the first war in which jet fighters met each other in combat.

US soldiers were sent to the Korean peninsula in the 1950s to protect South Korea from communist North Korea.

Wars against communism

The capitalist politics of the United States were the opposite of the Soviet Union's political system of communism. The two countries avoided direct war with each other but would often support the opposing sides in other wars. In 1950 North Korea, aided by the Soviet Union and China, attacked South Korea. Forces of the United Nations and the United States pushed the invaders back. Fighting continued until a ceasefire in 1953, but disputes still flare up there from time to time. North Korea has caused concern recently by developing nuclear weapons and the missiles to deliver them.

In the 1950s, communist uprisings in South Vietnam led to the United States's support for the anti-communist government. Terrorism and guerrilla warfare increased until full-scale war broke out between North Vietnam, with Soviet and Chinese support, and South Vietnam, supported by the United States. Despite pouring in troops and resources, it became clear that the United States could not win. US troops withdrew in 1973, and the South was taken over by the North in 1975.

In 1962, the United States learned that Soviet nuclear missiles had been placed in nearby Cuba. The world teetered on the brink of nuclear war for 13 days. In return for a US agreement not to invade Cuba and to remove missiles in Turkey, the Soviet Union agreed to remove its missiles from Cuba.

The US Army made extensive use of helicopters during the Vietnam War (1955–1975).

War in Afghanistan (1978–89)

In 1979, the Soviet Union sent troops to Afghanistan to support the pro-Soviet government, which had lost control of the country. Soviet troops fought rebel groups known as the mujahideen, who were supported by the United States. Despite occupying the country with more than 100,000 troops, the Soviets could not put down the rebellion. Unable to see any chance of victory, Soviet troops withdrew in 1989, leaving Afghanistan in a state of civil war and sowing the seeds of later Afghan wars. The 1979–1989 war has sometimes been described as the Soviet Union's Vietnam War.

Soviet helicopter gunships were very effective against mujahideen fighters until the United States supplied the mujahideen with heat-seeking Stinger missiles.

27

MODERN WARFARE
1980 – TODAY

SINCE 1980 THERE HAVE BEEN HUGE ADVANCES IN MILITARY TECHNOLOGY, INCLUDING UNMANNED AIRCRAFT AND STEALTH PLANES THAT ARE INVISIBLE TO RADAR. WARFARE HAS ALSO BECOME MORE ELECTRONIC, BASED ON COMPUTERS AND DIGITAL COMMUNICATIONS.

British Harrier 'Jump Jets' saw action against Argentinian Super Etendard fighters during the Falklands War in 1982.

Falklands War

On 2 April 1982, Argentinian troops invaded the Falkland Islands, a British territory in the South Atlantic Ocean. Three days later, Britain sent a naval task force to retake the islands. Fighting a war in such a remote location was difficult, but the British force fought its way across the islands and liberated them in just 74 days.

Yugoslav wars

Yugoslavia was created after World War II from six republics of Serbs, Croats, Bosnian Muslims, Albanians, Slovenes and others. In the 1990s tensions among the republics led to the nation's

a T-55 tank in service in Croatia

break-up as the republics started declaring their independence. The Yugoslav army tried to impose control in a series of wars. The North Atlantic Treaty Organisation (NATO) carried out bombing campaigns to protect civilians. With United Nations's help peace was restored in 2001.

Silent, invisible and deadly

Military developments since 1980 include cruise missiles. These highly accurate jet-engine powered missiles use satellite navigation to find their way. They can also compare the ground below them with a map that has been programmed into their memory to find a target.

The stealth plane uses its shapes, curves and edges to stay undetected on radar screens, so it is less likely to be attacked. The US B-2 bomber and F-117 Nighthawk are stealth planes.

Tomahawk cruise missiles can hit targets 2,500 km (1,553 miles) away.

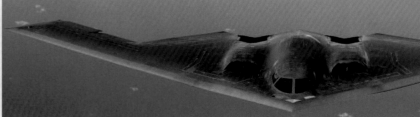

The B-2 bomber saw action for the first time in 1999 in Kosovo.

Afghanistan and Iraq

On 11 September 2001, '9/11', terrorists attacked the United States, killing 2,996 people. The US government demanded that Afghanistan hand over

US troops in Afghanistan could call in air support from ground attack aircraft.

Osama bin Laden, the leader of al-Qaeda, the group responsible for the attacks. When the Afghan government refused, a US-led force invaded and overthrew the government. Osama bin Laden was found in Pakistan in 2012 and killed by US forces.

In 2003, a US-led group invaded Iraq to remove its president, Saddam Hussein. Hussein was accused of committing brutal crimes against his people and of holding weapons of mass destruction (WMDs).

The decision was controversial because the approval of the United Nations had not been secured – and no WMDs were ever found. Hussein was captured and executed three years later.

Meanwhile, disputes between Iraqis and the occupying forces, and between Sunni and Shia Muslims, led to long-term conflicts and acts of terrorism. This gave rise to a new group, the Islamic State of Iraq and the Levant (ISIL), also known as IS or Daesh. Later the group spread into Syria.

The wars in Afghanistan and Iraq used infantry armed with rifles, artillery, tanks and air strikes. However, new technology – including satellite navigation, laser-guided weapons, stealth planes, supersonic jet-planes, remote-piloted aircraft and robots – was also employed.

For as long as the human need to defeat opponents continues, advances in technology will produce ever-smarter weapons to fight future wars.

Special forces worked secretly behind enemy lines.

The US AC-130 is a heavily armed gunship. It was developed from the C-130 Hercules, which was the workhorse of military air transport since the 1950s.

While the AC-130 has a crew of 13, other aircraft have no crew members onboard. They are the Unmanned Aerial Vehicles (UAVs), or drones.

The MQ-9 Reaper is one example, flown using remote control by a pilot on the ground via a satellite link. It can be armed with missiles or highly accurate laser-guided bombs.

The F-117 Nighthawk first flew in 1981.   *a Lockheed AC-130 gunship*   *Each MQ-9 Reaper costs about US$20 million.*

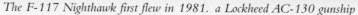

GLOSSARY

alliance
When several groups join and work together against one common enemy.

artillery
Large weapons that fire bigger bullets, balls and other projectiles much farther than handguns. Cannons were an early form of artillery.

bayonet
A knife or spike fixed to the end of a musket or similar gun barrel, so that the musket can be used as a spear or pike.

blitzkrieg
A sudden, intense, rapid attack using many kinds of weapons, highly mobile infantry, air support and other methods of assault.

breech-loaded
A firearm where the ball, bullet or other projectile is inserted in the breech or closed end, using some sort of temporary opening mechanism.

canister shot
Hollow cases or canisters filled with metal balls, nails or scrap iron, that smash apart when they hit the target to cause maximum physical damage.

cannon
A tube sealed at one end, with a charge of gunpowder at the sealed end to blast out any projectile such as a cannonball from the open end.

capitalism
A social system in which individuals manage trade and industry for profit.

cavalry
Soldiers or warriors who fight mainly on horseback.

chemical weapon
Harmful substance used in warfare, such as a poison gas, acid, and other dangerous liquids.

civil war
A war between two or more groups from the same country or nation.

Cold War
The rivalry between the United States and Soviet Union from after World War II to about 1990, when neither attacked each other, but supported opposing sides in other wars elsewhere.

combined arms
Using different weapons to achieve more than one kind of weapon could on its own.

communism
A social system in which a country's resources and assets are owned by everyone. In practice the system might be regulated by a single political party.

cruise missile
A jet-powered missile with a warhead that flies or 'cruises' a long distance to its target, controlled remotely by radio, or by its computer.

D-Day
The seaborne invasion carried out in World War II on 6 June 1944, by Allied forces.

drone
An unmanned aerial vehicle (UAV) controlled remotely by radio or with its own course and target programmed into its computer. Drones may carry out reconnaissance and/or use weapons such as guns and missiles.

firearm
A weapon that uses explosive force, such as from gunpowder, to shoot a projectile out of its barrel. Firearms are usually small and portable and used by one person.

Gatling gun
A gun with six or more barrels fixed to a central shaft. Turning a handle spins the barrels and fires each one once per revolution.

halberd
A pole with a metal spike and an axe-head on the end, used especially against opponents on horseback.

infantry
Soldiers or warriors who fight mainly on foot.

ironclad
A warship built of wood protected by an outer layer of metal armour, such as iron and, later, steel.

javelin
A lightweight spear designed mainly for throwing rather than thrusting or stabbing.

kamikaze mission
A suicide mission, in which the aircraft pilot or similar military person is expected to achieve their objective and then perish.

machine gun
A firearm that automatically fires many bullets or other projectiles in quick succession while the trigger is held.

missile
A rocket- or jet-powered flying weapon that carries a warhead and usually guides itself or is guided by remote control using radio signals.

musket
A long gun with a smooth inner bore, loaded at the muzzle (open end) and fired from the shoulder.

muzzle-loaded
A firearm where the ball, bullet or other projectile is inserted in the muzzle or open end.

NATO
North Atlantic Treaty Organization, a group of North American and European nations that agree to join forces to defend members who are attacked.

pike
A long pole with a sharp spear-tip, often used to fend off opponents on horseback.

reconnaissance
Finding out information, especially about an enemy, by various means such as spies, balloons, drones and listening in to phone calls, radio signals, computer lines and other communications.

rifling
Corkscrew grooves inside a firearm barrel that make a bullet or other projectile spin so that it travels farther and straighter.

siege
Surrounding and blockading or sealing off a castle, fort, city or other site, so that people or supplies cannot enter or leave.

stealth weapon
A plane, ship, missile or similar weapon that uses special shapes, curves, edges, paints, silencing and other features to stay undetected by the enemy, especially on radar screens.

surcoat
A sleeveless garment worn by a knight over armour, often embroidered with the knight's coat of arms.

U-boat
A submarine (a water craft that spends much of its time below the surface) used by German forces during World War I and World War II.

INDEX